MIKE'S
GAME STATION

By Barbara Hinyard

Illustrated by Abira Das

MIKE'S GAMESTATION

MIKE'S GAMESTATION © 2021 Barbara Hinyard

All rights reserved. This book or parts thereof may not be reproduced in any form, stored in a retrieval system, or transmitted in any form by any means—electronic, mechanical, photocopy, recording, or otherwise—without prior written permission of the publisher, except as provided by the United States of America copyright law.

ISBN: 9798743344710

Printed in the United States of America
First Edition:
Illustrations : Abira Das

Mike wants to learn about how to save and earn money

Mike's parents took him to the bank to open up his own bank account along with getting his first debit card.

Mike and his parents were sitting down at the table in the dining room eating dinner when he asked his mom and dad, "How can I buy a Game Station 5?"

Mom and Dad looked at Mike and said; if you want to buy a Game Station 5, you must work to earn it.

Well, son, you can earn money by doing chores around the house and cut your neighbors' grass. They need their grass cut.
Really Mike asked dad?
Yes, son! Dad said. How much is the Game Station son?
$300 dollars, dad!!!

I'll tell you what, Mike. If you can do the chores and cut your neighbors' grass on Saturdays, I will give you 20 dollars for doing the chores every Friday and you will charge your neighbors 10 dollars for cutting their grass for them. Does this sound like a deal, son?

Yes dad, thank you!!!

Chores List

1) Cutting grass

2) Putting away toys

3) Folding Laundry

Mike begins to do the chores around the house every day and cutting his neighbors grass every Saturday.

His parents gave him 20 dollars every Friday and his neighbors paid him 10 dollars for cutting the grass every Saturday.

Finally, Mike was ready to see how much money he saved up. Mom and dad, I'm ready to count my money and deposit it in the bank.

Mike's parents sat down with him and helped him count his money.

There's five Fridays in a month son.
Take $20 and multiple it by 5 you get what son?
$100.
That's right son.
Now do it again you have another set of $20 dollars now
multiple that by 5 and you get what son?

$100 dollars dad said mike!
You're correct said his dad.
Now add $100 plus 100 you get what?
$200 said mike.
You made $200 by doing chores.
Now let's count the money you made from cutting the grass
Sure dad said mike.
You made $10 cutting grass right son?
Right dad.
Let's multiple $10 time 10 because you cut the grass 10 Saturday's
What is $ 10 time 10
$100 dollars dad!! Said mike
Now take that $100 dollars and add it with $200 and you get what son?
$300 dollars dad!!! Said mike

He had $300 dollars saved up for his Game Station 5. He was ready to go deposit his 300 dollars in the bank.

The bank teller helped him fill out the form. Where do you want your $300 dollars to go, in your checking or saving?

Mike said, checking. That's right, son, a checking account is where you can use your debit card for anything you want besides depositing a check.

Today is the day the Game Station 5 will be in the store. Mom and dad, I'm ready to visit a Game Shop and buy my Game Station 5. Mike's parents drove him to a Game Shop to buy his Game Station 5.

That will be $300, said the cashier. Mike pulled out his debit card with 300 dollars on it.

Mom and dad, my hard work has paid off.
Mike said I told you, son; you must work hard
to get what you want in life.
No one is going to hand it to you. If you want
something, work for it.

Your mom and I wanted to teach you how to be responsible.
Thanks, mom and dad; you guys are the best!

Mike went home and began to play with his Game Station 5.

Mike's Currency

How much money does Mike have?
Help Mike count how much he saved up

Help Mike do his chores so that he can save up enough to buy the Game Station

Match the following